my itty-bitty bio

Anita Cameron

easterseals

Published in the United States of America by Cherry Lake Publishing Group
Ann Arbor, Michigan
www.cherrylakepublishing.com

Reading Adviser: Beth Walker Gambro, MS, Ed., Reading Consultant, Yorkville, IL
Book Designer: Jennifer Wahi
Illustrator: Jeff Bane

Photo Credits: © f11photo/Shutterstock, 5; © Anita Cameron, 7, 13; © ADAPT Museum, 9; © Tom Olin, 11, 15, 17, 22, 23; George H. W. Bush Presidential Photographs, The National Archives, 19; © Molly Riley/Alamy, 21

Cherry Lake Press is an imprint of Cherry Lake Publishing Group.

Library of Congress Cataloging-in-Publication Data

Names: Cameron, Anita, 1965- author. | Bane, Jeff, 1957- illustrator.
Title: Anita Cameron / by Anita Cameron, Jeff Bane.
Description: Ann Arbor, Michigan : Cherry Lake Publishing, [2023] | Series: My itty-bitty bio | Audience: Grades K-1 | Summary: "Anita Cameron, a disability rights advocate and activist, has moved the country closer to justice through her civil rights activism. This autobiography for early readers examines her life in a simple, age-appropriate way that helps young readers develop word recognition and reading skills. Developed in partnership with Easterseals and written by Anita Cameron herself, this title helps all readers learn from those who make a difference in our world. The My Itty-Bitty Bio series celebrates diversity, inclusion, and the values that readers of all ages can aspire to"-- Provided by publisher.
Identifiers: LCCN 2023009127 | ISBN 9781668927267 (hardcover) | ISBN 9781668928318 (paperback) | ISBN 9781668929780 (ebook) | ISBN 9781668931264 (pdf)
Subjects: LCSH: Cameron, Anita, 1965- | African American social reformers--New York (State)--Rochester--Biography--Juvenile literature. | African American women--New York (State)--Rochester--Biography--Juvenile literature. | African Americans with disabilities--Civil rights--Juvenile literature. | Civil rights movements--United States--History--Juvenile literature.
Classification: LCC HN65 .C356 2023 | DDC 303.48/4092--dc23/eng/20230417
LC record available at https://lccn.loc.gov/2023009127

Printed in the United States of America

table of contents

My Story 4

Timeline. 22

Glossary 24

Index 24

About the author: Anita Cameron is a writer, disability rights activist, and community organizer. She is the director of Minority Outreach at Not Dead Yet, a national disability rights organization that fights for people with disabilities. Anita lives in Rochester, New York, with her wife, Lisa, and cats, JoJo and Nemo.

About the illustrator: Jeff Bane and his two business partners own a studio along the American River in Folsom, California, home of the 1849 Gold Rush. When Jeff's not sketching or illustrating for clients, he's either swimming or kayaking in the river to relax.

About our partnership: This title was developed in partnership with Easterseals to support its mission of empowering people with disabilities. Through their national network of affiliates, Easterseals provides essential services and on-the-ground supports to more than 1.5 million people each year.

I was born in 1965 in Chicago.
I was born early. I almost died.

Where were you born?

I was blind. I had other **disabilities**. That did not stop me. I made a promise. I would make the world better.

I met Dennis Schreiber when I was 21. He was blind. He had other disabilities. He was like me. He worked to help people like us.

Wheelchair users cannot get up steps. Buses only had steps. Dennis and I joined a group to change that. It was called ADAPT.

How do you travel
from place to place?

We marched. We **protested**. We were peaceful. Sometimes we got arrested. I got arrested many times.

On March 13, 1990, I went to Washington, D.C. Many disabled people went. Leaders needed to know why **accessibility** was important. We showed them.

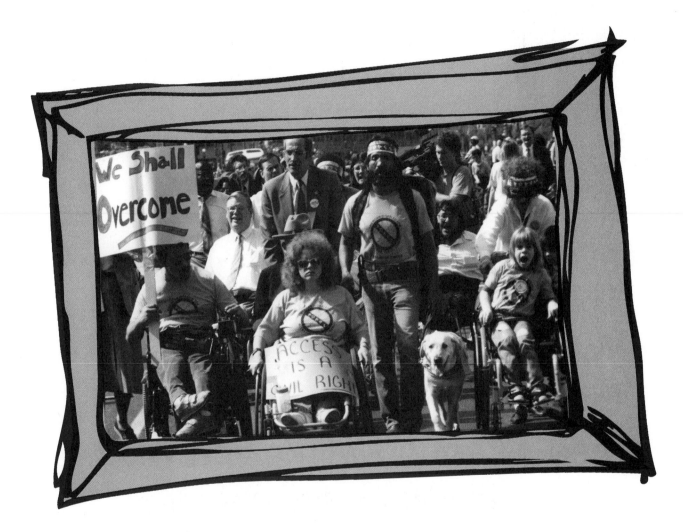

The **U.S. Capitol** has big steps. We crawled up. I carried my friend Frank's wheelchair. I got tired. I kept crawling. I crawled with my white cane. I helped other people up. I was proud.

The leaders saw what we did.
It helped them understand.
They passed the Americans with
Disabilities Act. This **law** helps
many people.

Today, I am a leader. I am a writer.
I still work for **justice**.

What would you like to ask me?

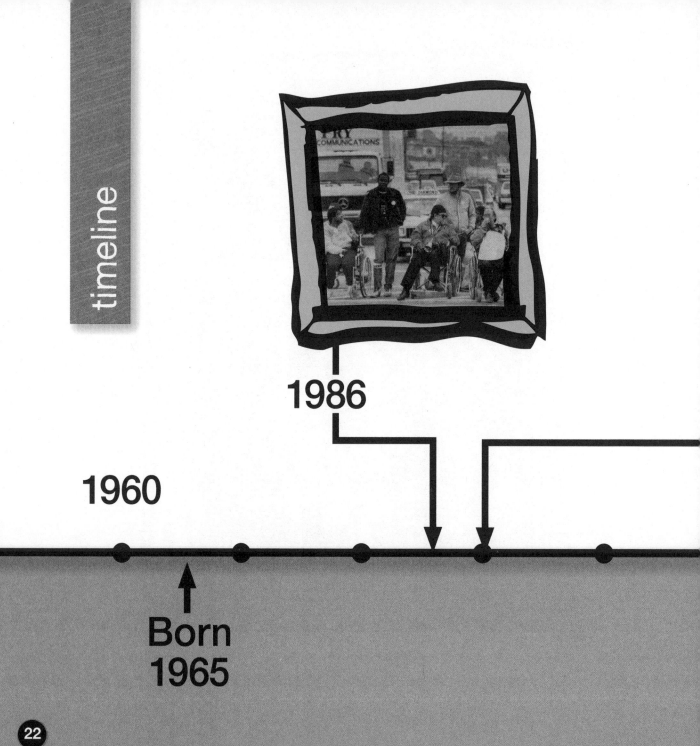

1986

1960

Born
1965

1990

2060

glossary

accessibility (eck-SESS-uh-bil-uh-tee) the practice of making places, information, or activities usable for everyone

disabilities (DIS-uh-bil-uh-tees) conditions that limit a person's movement, senses, or activities

justice (JUST-is) fair treatment under the law

law (LAW) an official rule put in place by a government

protested (PROH-test-uhd) expressed disapproval of systems or policies through words or actions

U.S. Capitol (YOO ES CAP-uh-tuhl) the building in Washington, D.C., where Congress works

index

accessibility, 10–11, 14–19

activism, 6, 8–18, 20–21

Americans with Disabilities Act (1990), 18–19

birth, 4–5, 22

blindness, 6–7, 8, 16

Chicago, 4–5

disabilities, 6, 8–11, 14–19

legislation, 18–19

public transportation, 10–11

Schreiber, Dennis, 8, 10

timeline, 22–23

U.S. Capitol, 14–19

wheelchair use, 9–11, 13–17, 19, 21